LESSONS FROM
THE QUR'AN

Mahmood Jawaid

Ta-Ha Publishers Ltd.
www.taha.co.uk

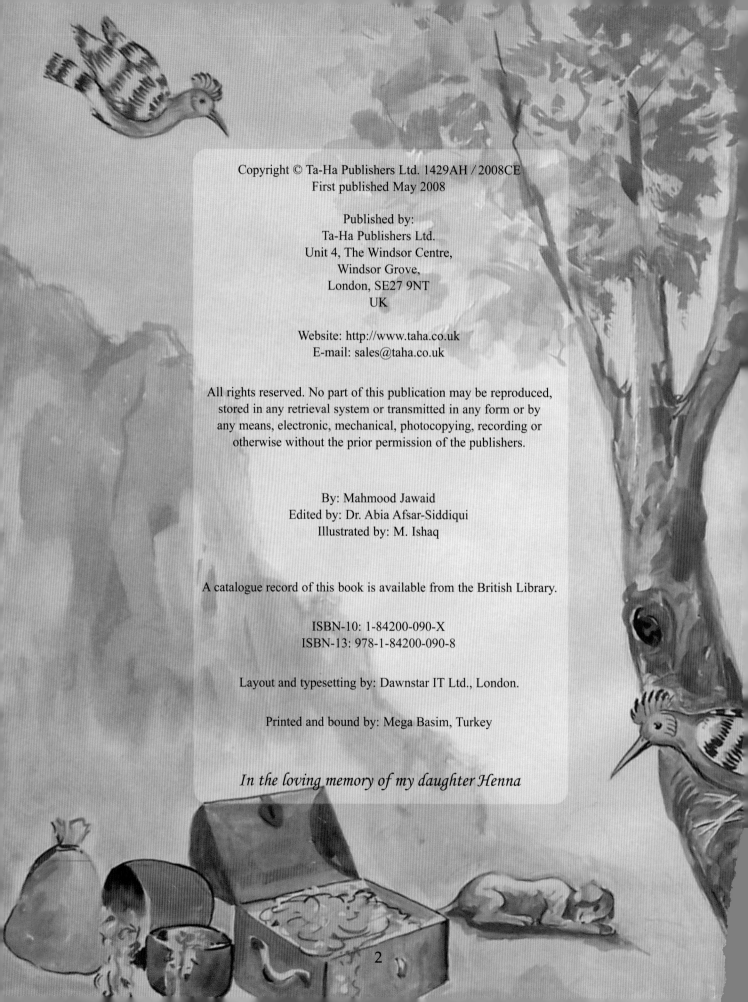

Published by:
Ta-Ha Publishers Ltd.
Unit 4, The Windsor Centre,
Windsor Grove,
London, SE27 9NT
UK

Website: http://www.taha.co.uk
E-mail: sales@taha.co.uk

By: Mahmood Jawaid
Edited by: Dr. Abia Afsar-Siddiqui
Illustrated by: M. Ishaq

A catalogue record of this book is available from the British Library.

ISBN-10: 1-84200-090-X
ISBN-13: 978-1-84200-090-8

Layout and typesetting by: Dawnstar IT Ltd., London.

Printed and bound by: Mega Basim, Turkey

In the loving memory of my daughter Henna

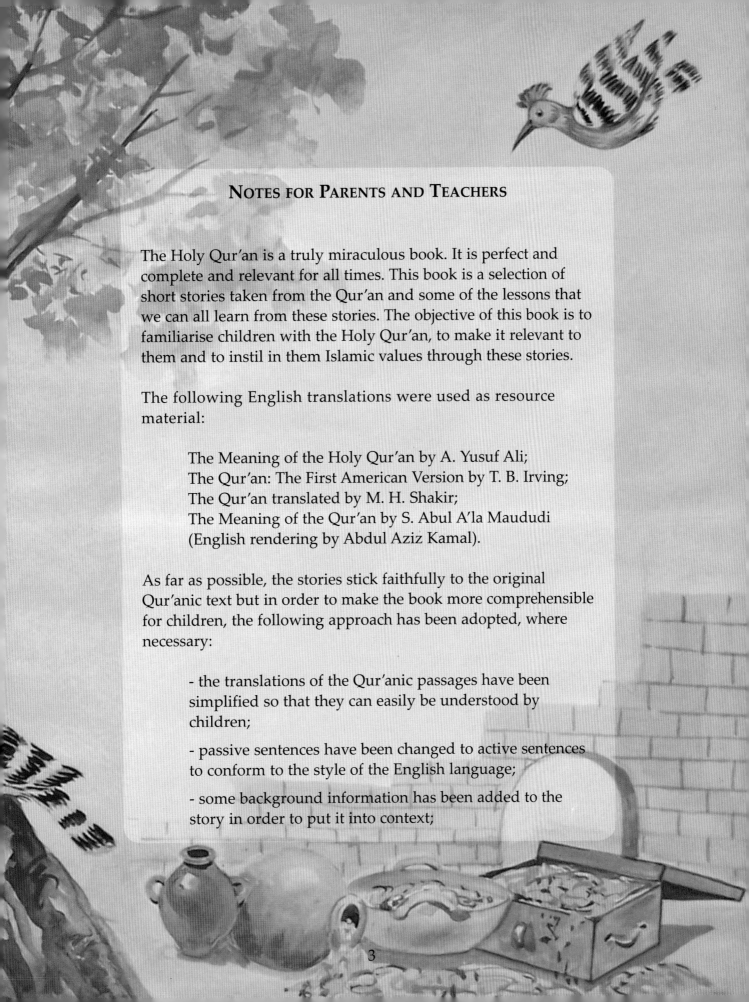

NOTES FOR PARENTS AND TEACHERS

The Holy Qur'an is a truly miraculous book. It is perfect and complete and relevant for all times. This book is a selection of short stories taken from the Qur'an and some of the lessons that we can all learn from these stories. The objective of this book is to familiarise children with the Holy Qur'an, to make it relevant to them and to instil in them Islamic values through these stories.

The following English translations were used as resource material:

> The Meaning of the Holy Qur'an by A. Yusuf Ali;
> The Qur'an: The First American Version by T. B. Irving;
> The Qur'an translated by M. H. Shakir;
> The Meaning of the Qur'an by S. Abul A'la Maududi
> (English rendering by Abdul Aziz Kamal).

As far as possible, the stories stick faithfully to the original Qur'anic text but in order to make the book more comprehensible for children, the following approach has been adopted, where necessary:

- the translations of the Qur'anic passages have been simplified so that they can easily be understood by children;

- passive sentences have been changed to active sentences to conform to the style of the English language;

- some background information has been added to the story in order to put it into context;

3

- the sequence of some sentences has been re-arranged and any gaps in the story have been filled in order to maintain the flow and the continuity of the story;

- repetitions and points of complexity have been excluded to keep the stories simple to understand.

The main lessons to be learned from the story are discussed after each story and presented in an easy-to-follow bullet-point format.

May Allah ﷻ make this book a bridge between children and the Holy Qur'an, guide them towards an Islamic way of life, and protect them from any harmful effects of this effort (ameen).

The following Arabic salutations have been used throughout the text:

ﷻ which is the Arabic for *subhanahu wa ta'ala*, meaning Glorious and Exalted is He. This is mentioned after the name of Allah alone.

ﷺ which is the Arabic for *sallallahu alayhi wa sallam*, meaning peace and blessings of Allah be upon him. This is always said after the name of the Prophet Muhammad ﷺ.

السلام which is the Arabic for *alayhi salaam*, meaning peace be upon him. This is always said after the names of the Prophets.

CONTENTS

THE ANGELS BOWED BUT SHAYTAN DISOBEYED

Al-Baqarah 2:30-34 and Al-'Araf 7:12-25

This book begins, appropriately, with the story of the creation of the first person on earth, Adam ﷺ. His story has been mentioned seven times in various places throughout the Qur'an. That is because it is a very interesting story and holds many lessons for us all if we read it carefully.

A long time ago Allah ﷻ gathered all the angels together and told them, "I am going to create an assistant *(Khalifah)* and put him on the Earth."

The angels said, "Are you going to create someone who will be mischievous and spill blood. Are we not enough to praise and glorify (worship) you?"

Allah ﷻ replied, "I know things that you do not know."

Once Allah ﷻ had made Adam ﷺ, He taught him the names of everything. Then Allah ﷻ presented those same things to the angels and said, "Tell me the names of these things if you are right."

The angels could not do this and replied, "Glory be to You! We do not know anything, except what you have taught us. You are Most Aware, Most Wise."

Then Allah ﷻ said to Adam علیه السلام, "O Adam, tell the angels the names of these things." And Adam علیه السلام did so.

Allah ﷻ said to the angels, "Did I not tell you that I know the secrets of the heavens and earth? I know what you reveal and what you hide. Now bow down before Adam."

They all bowed except a Jinn called Iblis. He refused to bow down to Adam علیه السلام.

Allah ﷻ said, "Why did you not bow to Adam when I ordered you to do so?"

Iblis replied, "I am better than him. You made me from fire and you made him from clay."

Allah ﷻ said angrily, "Get out of here. You have no right to be proud and arrogant about it. Get out! You are the lowest of created things."

Iblis said, "Give me permission until the Day of Judgement."

Allah ﷻ gave it to him, saying, "You have my permission."

Iblis said, "Since You have led me away from the Right Path, I will also lead Adam and his children away from the Right Path. I will attack them from the front, from behind, from the right and from the left. You will find that most of them will not be grateful to You for Your blessings."

So Allah ﷻ said to Iblis, "Get out of here, you will be hated and rejected. If any of the children of Adam follow you, then I will fill Hell with all of you."

Allah ﷻ then said to Adam ﷺ, "O Adam! Live in Paradise with your wife. Eat anything that you like from here, but do not go near this tree, because that will harm you."

The Shaytan did not like the fact that Adam ﷺ and his wife, Hawwa, were living in Paradise. He wanted them out of there and he knew that if they ate from the forbidden tree then they would be thrown out of Paradise. So he started putting false ideas in their minds saying, "Do you know why Allah does not want you to eat from this tree? He does not want you two to become angels. He does not want you two to live forever."

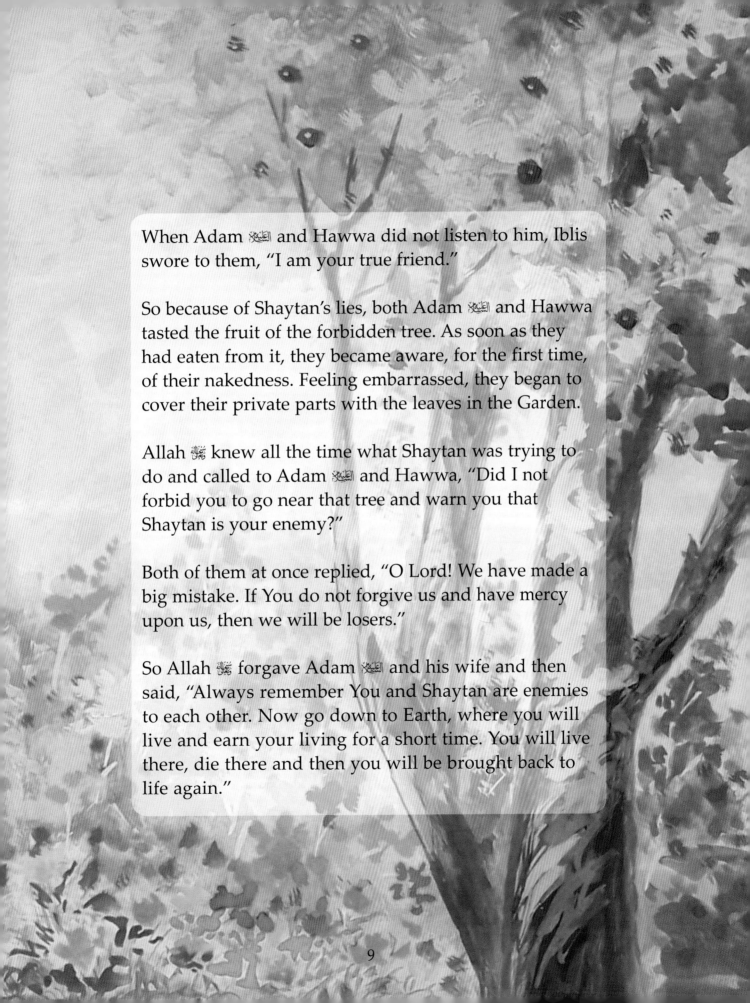

When Adam ﷺ and Hawwa did not listen to him, Iblis swore to them, "I am your true friend."

So because of Shaytan's lies, both Adam ﷺ and Hawwa tasted the fruit of the forbidden tree. As soon as they had eaten from it, they became aware, for the first time, of their nakedness. Feeling embarrassed, they began to cover their private parts with the leaves in the Garden.

Allah ﷻ knew all the time what Shaytan was trying to do and called to Adam ﷺ and Hawwa, "Did I not forbid you to go near that tree and warn you that Shaytan is your enemy?"

Both of them at once replied, "O Lord! We have made a big mistake. If You do not forgive us and have mercy upon us, then we will be losers."

So Allah ﷻ forgave Adam ﷺ and his wife and then said, "Always remember You and Shaytan are enemies to each other. Now go down to Earth, where you will live and earn your living for a short time. You will live there, die there and then you will be brought back to life again."

LESSONS TO BE LEARNED

- Allah ﷻ made Adam ﷺ His assistant on earth and we, as the children of Adam, are also Allah's assistants on earth.

- Being an assistant of Allah ﷻ on earth means that we have control over many things and we have a choice of what to do. For example, we can use our tongues to either say good words that will make people happy or to say bad words that can hurt people. We can use our hands to help people or we can use them to harm people and destroy the things around us.

- With this choice, we also have a responsibility and we have to answer to Allah ﷻ about what we have done here on earth. This will happen on the Day of Judgement, when we will be brought back to life after we have died. If we have done good deeds then Allah ﷻ will reward us, but if we have made bad choices, then Allah ﷻ may punish us.

- The angels knew that many people would not make the right choices and be mischievous, but what they did not know is that Allah ﷻ also gave us all wisdom and knowledge. We should use these to tell us what is right and what is wrong. Angels do not have this choice, so when Allah ﷻ asked them to bow down, they all bowed.

- Iblis, the real name of Shaytan, refused to bow because he was too proud and thought that he was better than Adam عليه السلام. We should never act proud and arrogant. Allah ﷻ does not like arrogant and mean people. We should never think that we are better than anyone, because Allah ﷻ made us all with our unique strengths and weaknesses.

- Shaytan is our worst enemy. He does not want anyone to go to Paradise because he was thrown out of there. He tricked Adam عليه السلام and Hawwa into eating the fruit of the tree which Allah ﷻ had forbidden and got them expelled from Paradise. Even today, he is still trying to trick us by always trying to put bad thoughts in our minds.

- Our real home is Paradise, where Adam عليه السلام and Hawwa were living when Allah ﷻ created them. We can go back to our real home by following the orders of Allah ﷻ and refusing to act upon bad ideas put in our mind by Iblis.

- As soon as Adam عليه السلام and Hawwa ate from the tree, they became aware of their private parts, which were previously hidden from them. They became embarrassed and tried to cover themselves up. We should always cover our private parts except when it is necessary.

- When Adam عليه السلام and Hawwa realised that they had disobeyed Allah ﷻ by eating the fruit, they immediately asked Allah ﷻ to forgive them. When we make a mistake and we realise it, we should immediately ask Allah ﷻ to forgive us. We should have the intention of not making the same mistake again.

THE DEAD COME BACK TO LIFE

Al-Baqarah 2:259-260

*We have seen in the previous story that we will have to answer to Allah
ﷻ about what we did here on earth. After we die, then we will be
brought back to life again on the Day of Judgement and asked about our
lives on earth. It is difficult to imagine that anything can come to life
after it has died but there are examples in the Qur'an showing that
Allah ﷻ can do anything including bringing the dead back to life.*

One day a man was travelling through a town on his
donkey. But there was nobody living in the town. There
were no people there and all the buildings were in
ruins.

Since he had been travelling for a long time, the man
was tired. He decided to lie down under a tree. He laid
his food on one side and tied his donkey to the tree on
the other side. While lying down he thought to himself,
"How will Allah ﷻ ever bring this town back to life?"
He then fell asleep.

Instead of waking up the next day, he kept on
sleeping for one hundred years, after which time he
woke up. When he woke up he thought that he had
had a short nap.

Allah ﷻ then asked the man, "How long have you been sleeping?"

The man replied, "I may have been sleeping for a day or maybe half a day."

Allah ﷻ said, "No! You have been sleeping for one hundred years. Look at your food and drink. Even after all this time they still look fresh. Now look at your donkey. The only things left of it are bones. Now watch how I put these bones together and then put muscle and skin around them."

The man watched intently. Just as Allah ﷻ had said, the bones of the donkey came together and then the muscle and flesh were wrapped around the bones and finally the skin. The donkey became alive again.

When the man saw this miracle of Allah ﷻ, he said, "I know for certain that Allah ﷻ is All-Powerful and can do anything."

13

The other story is about the Prophet Ibrahim ﷺ, who believed in Allah ﷻ, in the Day of Judgement and in Life after Death. But still he used to wonder how Allah ﷻ would bring people back to life on the Day of Judgement.

So one day Ibrahim ﷺ asked Allah ﷻ, "O Allah, show me how you give life to the dead."

Allah ﷻ said, "What? Do you not believe in Life after Death?"

Ibrahim ﷺ said, "Of course I do, but I really want to see how You do it, so that I can be completely satisfied."

Allah ﷻ said, "Alright! Take four birds and train them to follow your orders. Then slaughter them all, cut them into pieces, mix them up and spread their parts all around the mountain. Then call them. You will see that they will come flying to you."

So Ibrahim ﷺ took four birds and trained them well. When they were well trained to follow his orders, he slaughtered them all and cut them into small pieces and spread their parts all around the mountain. He then started calling them. He saw all the parts of each bird coming together from different parts of the mountain. All the birds had become alive again before Ibrahim's ﷺ eyes.

Ibrahim ﷺ was amazed at what he saw and he truly understood that Allah ﷻ is All-Wise and All-Powerful.

LESSONS TO BE LEARNED

- Even if it seems impossible to do, Allah ﷻ can do anything. It is an important part of our faith that we believe that we will be brought back to life on the Day of Judgement, just as the donkey and the birds were brought back to life by Allah ﷻ after they had died.

- We may not be able to see dead animals come back to life because Allah ﷻ showed these special miracles to special people like the Prophets.

- However, there are lots of Allah's miracles all around for us to see. For example, look carefully at a tree. It is green and full of life in summer. Then when autumn comes, all the leaves turn different colours and fall off the tree, so that by the time winter comes, the tree looks dead and bare. Then we see buds and fresh green leaves in the spring and the tree has come back to life, by the permission of Allah ﷻ.

The other miracle was that after one hundred years, the donkey had died and only its bones were left. But the food and drink that the traveller had were still fresh after one hundred years. This shows us again that Allah ﷻ can do anything He wishes. We may not understand why something has happened but we believe in the Power of Allah ﷻ.

THE PEOPLE OF THE CAVE
(ASHABUL-KAHF)

Al-Kahf 18:9-22

We have just read the story of a man who slept for one hundred years and then woke up by the permission of Allah ﷻ. This is the story of another group of special people called the People of the Cave, or Ashabul-Kahf in Arabic, who also slept for hundreds of years.

Long before the time of the Prophet Muhammad ﷺ, there were a group of intelligent and pious young men who only worshipped Allah ﷻ. Some people say that there were three young men, some say there were five, and some say there were seven. Nobody knows how many young men there were, except Allah ﷻ and a few special people. But what we do know for certain is that they had a dog with them.

These young men lived in a place where nobody worshipped Allah ﷻ. In fact the king at that time did not like people who worshipped Allah ﷻ and would punish them.

But the young men were not afraid of the king and bravely used to tell the people where they lived, "We only worship Allah ﷻ who is the Lord of the Heavens and Earth. If we worship anything other than Allah ﷻ, then we will be making a big mistake. Our people worship other gods. If they are right then let them prove it."

The people did not like hearing this and started to make life difficult for the young men. Finally, the young men decided to leave the town and took shelter in a nearby cave. They had full trust in Allah ﷻ and prayed to Him, "O Allah! Have mercy on us and find a good solution for us."

So the young men settled in the cave confident that Allah ﷻ would protect them. When night fell, they went to sleep. Years passed but they did not wake up. Everyday Allah ﷻ would turn them to the right and to the left, so that they would be comfortable. The cave was in such a position that the sun would rise on the right side of the cave and would set on the left side, but there was never any sunlight inside the cave. This meant that no one could see inside the cave to disturb the sleepers and also that the cave was cool and comfortable to sleep in during the hot days. It was dark inside and Allah ﷻ even sealed the ears of the young men so that they could sleep in peace. The dog slept at the mouth of the cave guarding it and all this was such a scary sight that anyone who dared to come close ran away in fright.

This is how Allah ﷻ protected the *Ashabul-Kahf* from those that wanted to harm them and they slept like this for three hundred and nine years.

At long last the young men awoke and one of them asked, "How long have we been sleeping?"

Another replied, "Perhaps we have been sleeping for a day or half of a day."

Yet another young man said, "Allah knows best. At the moment, one of us should go to the nearest town and buy some good and pure food. But make sure no one finds out about us, because if they do, they will force us to worship their gods or kill us if we don't."

The young men thought that nothing in the place around them had changed including the bad king and the people that had tried to harm them before they went into the cave. They thought that they had slept for a day at most and never imagined that they had been asleep for over three hundred years.

When one of the *Ashabul-Kahf* went into town to buy some food, he found that everything had changed; his clothes were different, the way he spoke was different and the money he used to buy food with was no longer in use. The people of the town were amazed to see such a person and were interested in his story. The town people told the young man that the people who did not worship Allah ﷻ were long dead. The people that were now living in the town worshipped Allah ﷻ and that they had a good king.

It was then that the *Ashabul-Kahf* realised that they had been asleep for centuries and they were thankful to Allah ﷻ that their enemies were long dead and that the people now worshipped Allah ﷻ.

LESSONS TO BE LEARNED

- The young men were surrounded by people who made their life difficult and teased them for worshipping Allah ﷻ. But they were not afraid to speak the truth and were only afraid of Allah ﷻ. When we are teased for being a good Muslim, we should never be afraid of other people who make fun of us or disobey Allah ﷻ or stop doing the right thing.

- When life became very difficult for the young men, they asked for Allah's ﷻ help and protection. If we have the right intention in our heart and pray to Allah ﷻ then Allah ﷻ will protect us when we need it just as He protected the People of the Cave.

- The People of the Cave had faith and trusted in Allah ﷻ and prayed to him, so Allah ﷻ made things easy for them. We should have complete trust in Allah ﷻ at all times, not only the easy and comfortable times but also the difficult times.

- In this world, nothing lasts forever. If we are patient then even bad situations can change to good ones, by the permission of Allah ﷻ; for example, the city where the *Ashabul-Kahf* lived became a city full of people who worshipped Allah ﷻ.

- We should not argue with other people about things that do not matter. When the young men woke up, they asked each other about how long they had been sleeping. One of them answered, "Allah knows best." When we do not know the answer to something then instead of arguing about it, it is better to say, "Allah knows best."

THE WICKED PHARAOH

Al-'Araf 7:103-137

There have been many kings and rulers throughout history that made life difficult for people who worshipped Allah ﷻ alone. The one most often mentioned in the Qur'an is the Pharaoh of Egypt, whose story has been told in great detail. He was a wicked man who thought that he was like a god. Allah ﷻ sent the Prophet Musa ﷺ to show him the Right Way.

Pharaoh was a wicked man. He thought that because he was king, he could do what he liked. One day the Prophet Musa ﷺ came to him and said, "O Pharaoh! I am a prophet from Allah and I want to tell you about the religion of Allah. I have a sign proving that I am a prophet."

The Pharaoh replied, "If you are telling the truth, then show me the sign."

Musa ﷺ threw the stick he was carrying on the ground, and by the permission of Allah ﷻ, it became a serpent. Then Musa ﷺ took his hand out from underneath his cloak and it dazzled with white light.

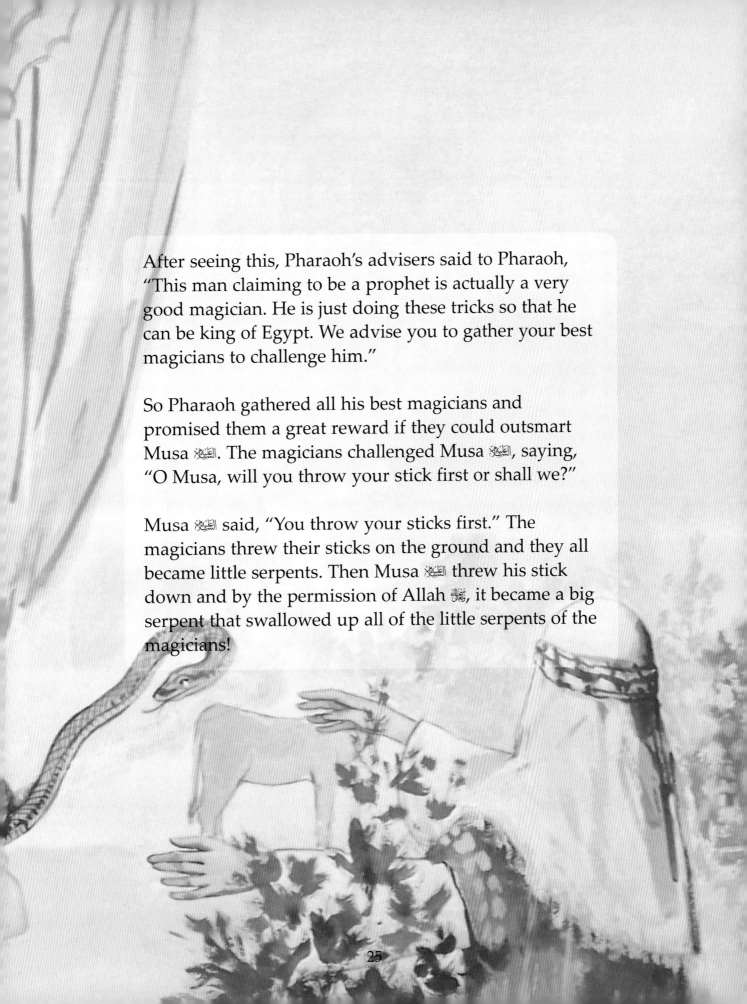

After seeing this, Pharaoh's advisers said to Pharaoh, "This man claiming to be a prophet is actually a very good magician. He is just doing these tricks so that he can be king of Egypt. We advise you to gather your best magicians to challenge him."

So Pharaoh gathered all his best magicians and promised them a great reward if they could outsmart Musa عليه السلام. The magicians challenged Musa عليه السلام, saying, "O Musa, will you throw your stick first or shall we?"

Musa عليه السلام said, "You throw your sticks first." The magicians threw their sticks on the ground and they all became little serpents. Then Musa عليه السلام threw his stick down and by the permission of Allah ﷻ, it became a big serpent that swallowed up all of the little serpents of the magicians!

This proved that Musa ﷺ was telling the truth and all the magicians fell down to the ground bowing in *sajdah* saying, "We believe in Allah, the Lord of the Universe and the Lord of Musa and Harun."

Pharaoh became angry and said, "How can you believe in Allah when I have not given you permission to do so? Don't you know that this is a trick of Musa and that he is planning to get rid of us all? If you continue to believe in Allah then I will cut off your hands and feet and hang you on the cross."

But the magicians were firm in their belief and refused to listen to the Pharaoh, saying, "We will return to Allah ﷻ. But will you punish us for believing in the signs of Allah ﷻ?" Then they prayed, "O Allah! Give us patience and let us die as Muslims."

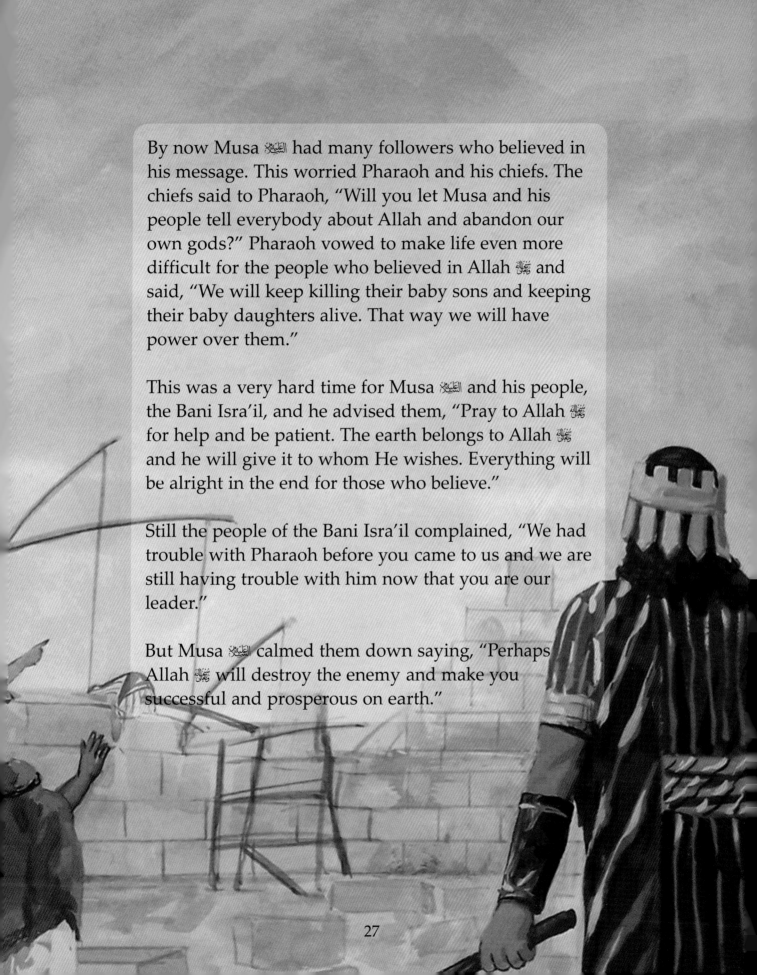

By now Musa ﷺ had many followers who believed in his message. This worried Pharaoh and his chiefs. The chiefs said to Pharaoh, "Will you let Musa and his people tell everybody about Allah and abandon our own gods?" Pharaoh vowed to make life even more difficult for the people who believed in Allah ﷻ and said, "We will keep killing their baby sons and keeping their baby daughters alive. That way we will have power over them."

This was a very hard time for Musa ﷺ and his people, the Bani Isra'il, and he advised them, "Pray to Allah ﷻ for help and be patient. The earth belongs to Allah ﷻ and he will give it to whom He wishes. Everything will be alright in the end for those who believe."

Still the people of the Bani Isra'il complained, "We had trouble with Pharaoh before you came to us and we are still having trouble with him now that you are our leader."

But Musa ﷺ calmed them down saying, "Perhaps Allah ﷻ will destroy the enemy and make you successful and prosperous on earth."

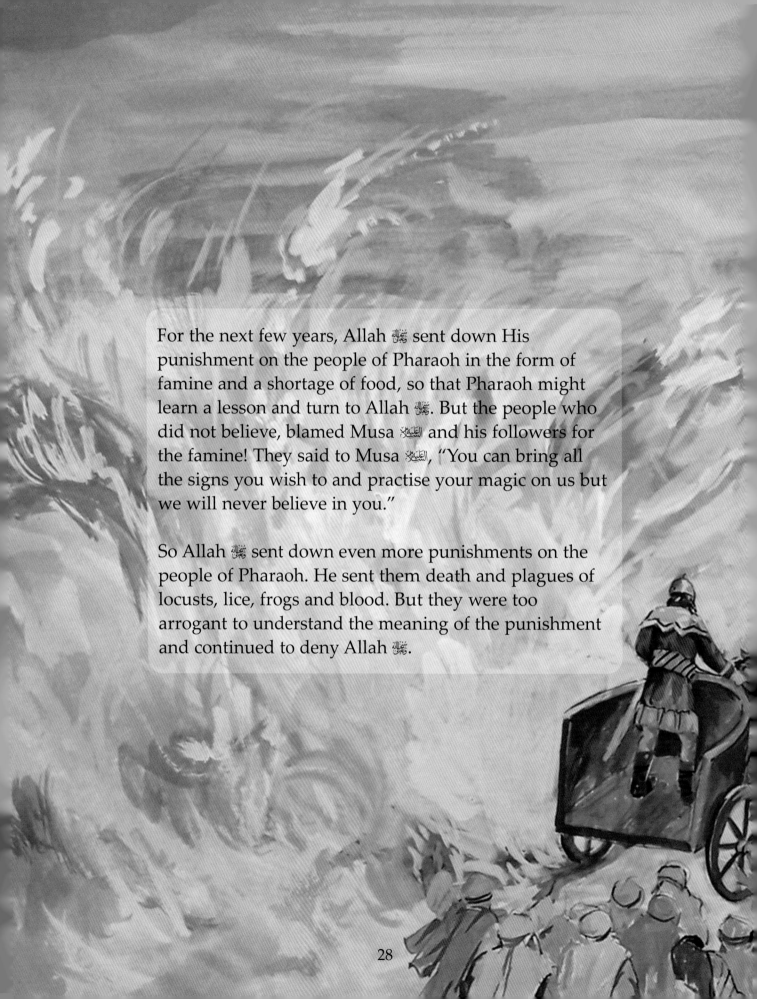

For the next few years, Allah ﷻ sent down His punishment on the people of Pharaoh in the form of famine and a shortage of food, so that Pharaoh might learn a lesson and turn to Allah ﷻ. But the people who did not believe, blamed Musa عليه السلام and his followers for the famine! They said to Musa عليه السلام, "You can bring all the signs you wish to and practise your magic on us but we will never believe in you."

So Allah ﷻ sent down even more punishments on the people of Pharaoh. He sent them death and plagues of locusts, lice, frogs and blood. But they were too arrogant to understand the meaning of the punishment and continued to deny Allah ﷻ.

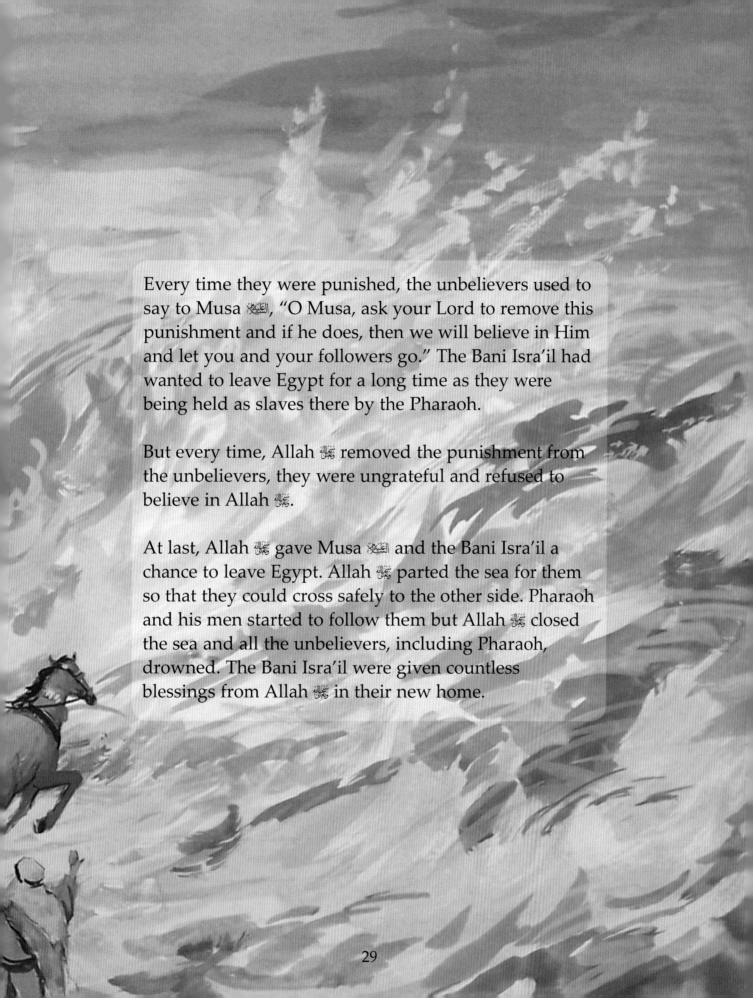

Every time they were punished, the unbelievers used to say to Musa ﷺ, "O Musa, ask your Lord to remove this punishment and if he does, then we will believe in Him and let you and your followers go." The Bani Isra'il had wanted to leave Egypt for a long time as they were being held as slaves there by the Pharaoh.

But every time, Allah ﷻ removed the punishment from the unbelievers, they were ungrateful and refused to believe in Allah ﷻ.

At last, Allah ﷻ gave Musa ﷺ and the Bani Isra'il a chance to leave Egypt. Allah ﷻ parted the sea for them so that they could cross safely to the other side. Pharaoh and his men started to follow them but Allah ﷻ closed the sea and all the unbelievers, including Pharaoh, drowned. The Bani Isra'il were given countless blessings from Allah ﷻ in their new home.

LESSONS TO BE LEARNED

- Allah ﷻ granted Pharaoh power and wealth in this world, but he was too proud and ungrateful to Allah ﷻ. Instead of using his power to do good things, he used it to hurt the people who believed in Allah ﷻ, the Bani Isra'il. This made Allah ﷻ angry, but Allah ﷻ does not punish wicked people straight away. He gives them a chance to repent, change their ways and believe in Him because He is All-Kind and All-Merciful.

- Allah ﷻ sent a series of small punishments to Pharaoh and his people as a warning, so that they might change. But they were not intelligent enough to understand that the punishments were a warning from Allah ﷻ. So Allah ﷻ finally sent a big punishment to Pharaoh and drowned him and his followers in the sea. People who are wicked and ignore the signs of Allah ﷻ are punished in this world and also thrown into Hell on the Day of Judgement.

- When Musa عليه السلام showed his signs to Pharaoh and his magicians, the magicians used their intelligence and believed in Allah ﷻ straight away. We should also use our intelligence and common sense to tell us what is right and wrong.

- The magicians who believed in Allah ﷻ were not frightened when Pharaoh threatened to kill them. They asked Allah ﷻ for patience. When the Bani Isra'il were in difficulties, Musa عليه السلام advised them to ask Allah ﷻ for patience. Patience is a very difficult thing for people to have unless they have very strong belief in Allah ﷻ. Whenever we are in difficulty then we should also ask for patience from Allah ﷻ. That will help us to get through any hard times.

THE RICH QARUN

Al-Qasas 28:76-82

This is the story of a man who lived during the time of Musa ﷺ and we shall see what happened to him because he was too proud and arrogant about all his wealth.

During the time of Musa ﷺ, there lived in Egypt a man named Qarun. Qarun had so much wealth that even the keys to his numerous treasure chests had to be carried by dozens of strong men. He was very proud of his wealth and his people would warn him, "Do not be proud of your wealth because Allah ﷻ does not love those who are proud of their riches. Instead use the wealth that Allah ﷻ has given you to help you in the Hereafter. The way to do this is to spend your money in charity and do good works. Allah ﷻ has been good to you so you should be good to others. Do not be a troublemaker because Allah ﷻ doesn't like troublemakers."

Qarun replied arrogantly, "I am rich because I am clever." He did not think that his wealth was a blessing from Allah ﷻ. He was forgetting that Allah ﷻ had destroyed many people before him who were stronger and richer than he was. So why wasn't he punished straight away for his arrogance? Because Allah ﷻ does

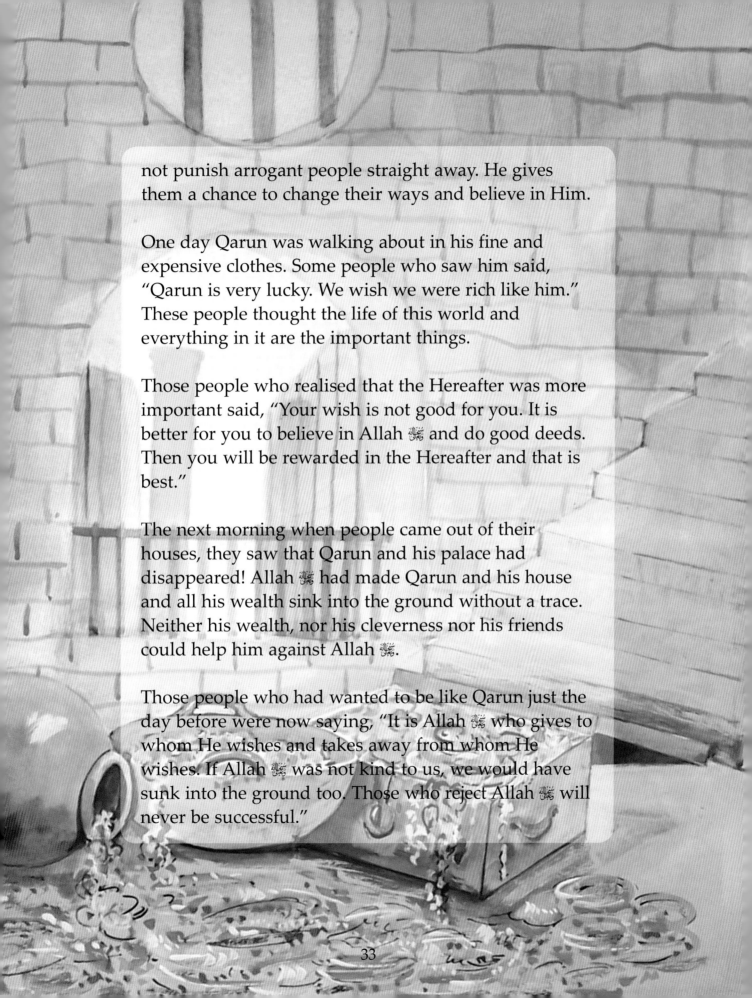

not punish arrogant people straight away. He gives them a chance to change their ways and believe in Him.

One day Qarun was walking about in his fine and expensive clothes. Some people who saw him said, "Qarun is very lucky. We wish we were rich like him." These people thought the life of this world and everything in it are the important things.

Those people who realised that the Hereafter was more important said, "Your wish is not good for you. It is better for you to believe in Allah ﷻ and do good deeds. Then you will be rewarded in the Hereafter and that is best."

The next morning when people came out of their houses, they saw that Qarun and his palace had disappeared! Allah ﷻ had made Qarun and his house and all his wealth sink into the ground without a trace. Neither his wealth, nor his cleverness nor his friends could help him against Allah ﷻ.

Those people who had wanted to be like Qarun just the day before were now saying, "It is Allah ﷻ who gives to whom He wishes and takes away from whom He wishes. If Allah ﷻ was not kind to us, we would have sunk into the ground too. Those who reject Allah ﷻ will never be successful."

LESSONS TO BE LEARNED

● Our possessions are a gift from Allah ﷻ, not because of our talents or knowledge. Allah ﷻ gives to whom He wishes and He can also take away from whom He wishes at any time.

● If Allah ﷻ has blessed us with wealth, then we should not be proud and arrogant about it and we should not think that we are better than other people because of what we have.

● Wealth is a test from Allah ﷻ. He wants to see how we use it. If we thank Allah ﷻ for the wealth, fulfil our basic needs and share the rest with the poor and needy then we have passed the test. The reward is Paradise in the Hereafter, insha'Allah.

● If we waste our wealth, act smug, show off, or feel proud to be rich then we have failed the test. Allah ﷻ may not punish us straight away. But the punishment will eventually come and then nothing and no one can help us. Allah ﷻ may not only take our wealth away from us, He may destroy us and our home and we may be punished in the Hereafter.

- We should not be jealous of rich people. Allah ﷻ also tests us by giving us too little, or just enough. If we complain or do not thank Allah ﷻ then we have failed the test. If we thank Allah ﷻ and still share with the poor then we have passed the test.

- Whether we are rich or poor, we should always believe in Allah ﷻ, thank him for whatever He has given to us, and do good deeds. Then Allah ﷻ will reward us on the Day of Judgement, insha'Allah. The reward on the Day of Judgement is the best reward anyone can have, better than anything in this world.

- Qarun thought that he was clever. But someone who does not believe in Allah ﷻ cannot be clever. The most intelligent person is the person who believes in Allah ﷻ and obeys His commands. The person with the most knowledge is the person who knows and understands most about Islam. Being intelligent and knowledgeable is better than having lots of money.

THE BOASTFUL GARDENER

Al-Kahf 18:32-44

This is another story about a rich person who thought that he was better than a poor person. He thought that he became rich because he was clever, but he did not believe in Allah ﷻ.

Once upon a time there were two gardeners. One gardener was very rich. Allah ﷻ had given him two gardens of grapevines that were surrounded with date palms. In between the two gardens there was a big cornfield and a flowing river. Both of these gardens produced a lot of fruit.

One day the rich gardener was going to his gardens. On his way he met a poor gardener and started boasting to him, "I am richer and more powerful than you. Everybody listens to me."

As he was talking, they both entered the garden. The rich gardener continued to boast, "I do not think that this garden will ever be destroyed. I do not believe in the Day of Judgement. Even if there is a Day of Judgement and I am brought back to life, I will get more money and more power there than I have now."

The poor gardener, who had been listening to the boasting, said, "Do you not believe in Allah ﷻ, who created you from dust and made you into a man? I believe in Allah ﷻ and I do not make anyone equal to Him. When you entered your garden, why did you not say: *'Masha'Allah, la quwwata illa billah* - Whatever Allah wishes happens, there is no power except the power of Allah.' I may not be rich as you are. I may have fewer children than you have. But Allah ﷻ may give me something better than your two gardens. What would you do if Allah ﷻ sent a thunderbolt from the sky? Then your garden will be ruined and covered with water and you will not even be able to find it."

And so it happened. The rich gardener's wealth was destroyed and his gardens were ruined.

When he saw this, the boastful gardener was very upset. He had spent all his money on his garden and now there was nothing left of it. All the people that he thought he had power over could not help him, all the money he had could not help him; only Allah ﷻ can protect and reward and give success. All he could say was, "I should never have associated anyone with Allah ﷻ."

Lessons to be Learned

- The rich gardener boasted to his poor companion about how rich and powerful he was and how he thought that this would last forever. He did not realise that whatever we have or own is a blessing and a mercy from Allah ﷻ. He can either bless us and give us more or He can take it back whenever He wishes. It is nothing to do with how clever or talented we are.

- The boastful gardener thought he was better than the poor gardener because he had more wealth and children. But in fact, the poor gardener was a better person because he believed in Allah ﷻ.

- The poor gardener was not impressed by the rich gardener's wealth and was not afraid to tell him the truth. Muslims do not judge people by how much money or power they have. Just because someone is rich or has more things, it does not mean that Allah ﷻ favours him or that he is better than other people. We should never look down on other people or think we are better than them. Only Allah ﷻ knows who is a better person.

- Allah ﷻ is always testing us. He can test us by giving us too much, too little or just enough.

- If we have been given lots of blessings from Allah ﷻ then we should say, *Masha'Allah, la quwwata illa billah*, which means: Whatever Allah wishes happens, there is no power except the power of Allah. We should always be thankful to Allah ﷻ for what He has given us and use it to help other people. If we do that then we have passed the test and Allah ﷻ will, insha'Allah, bless us more. If we show off and are proud, then we have failed the test and Allah ﷻ may take away what we have.

- If we think we have been given less blessings of Allah ﷻ, then we should still be thankful and show patience and share what we have with other people. If we do that then we have passed the test and Allah ﷻ will increase our blessings, insha'Allah. If we complain and are ungrateful then we have failed the test and Allah ﷻ will not bless us.

THE GREEDY GARDENERS

Al-Qalam 68:17-33

This is a similar story about some greedy gardeners, who did not want to share their wealth with the poor and needy in case there was less for themselves. But Allah 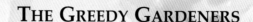 had another plan for them.

Once upon a time there were some gardeners. They were very rich but they were also very stingy, so Allah decided to test them. In one season He gave them lots of fruits in their garden. Since they were mean, they did not want to share these fruits with the poor people and so they decided to go out early the next morning and pick off all the fruit from the trees so the poor people could not have it. While they were talking about their plan, they did not say *insha'Allah* which means 'If Allah wishes'.

That night while the gardeners were asleep, there was a terrible storm that blew down all the trees and destroyed all the fruits.

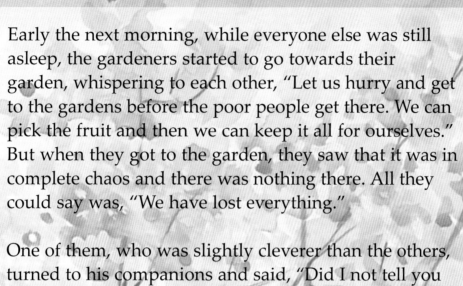

Early the next morning, while everyone else was still asleep, the gardeners started to go towards their garden, whispering to each other, "Let us hurry and get to the gardens before the poor people get there. We can pick the fruit and then we can keep it all for ourselves." But when they got to the garden, they saw that it was in complete chaos and there was nothing there. All they could say was, "We have lost everything."

One of them, who was slightly cleverer than the others, turned to his companions and said, "Did I not tell you that we should thank Allah ﷻ?"

The other gardeners realised their mistake and said, "Praise be to Allah ﷻ. We have been wrong."

Then they started blaming each other and saying, "Shame on us. We were very greedy. Let us pray to Allah ﷻ to forgive us. He may give us a better garden if we do good deeds and ask for forgiveness."

LESSONS TO BE LEARNED

- Allah ﷻ has commanded the rich to share their wealth with the poor. The greedy gardeners tried to disobey this command of Allah ﷻ and that is why they were punished. They were being mean about a few fruits, so Allah ﷻ took away all their fruits from them to teach them a lesson.

- We should always be generous when we give. This does not mean that we will have less for ourselves because Allah ﷻ will always give us more. But if we do not share what we have with those who need it more than we do, then Allah ﷻ has the power to take away everything from us.

- While they were making plans, the gardeners should have said *insha'Allah* which means 'If Allah wishes'. We should always remember that nothing can happen unless Allah 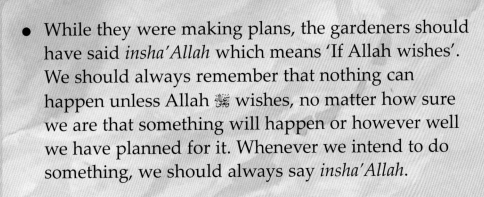 wishes, no matter how sure we are that something will happen or however well we have planned for it. Whenever we intend to do something, we should always say *insha'Allah*.

- As soon as the gardeners found out that they had done something bad, they asked for forgiveness from Allah. When we have done something wrong, then we should stop it straight away, ask Allah to forgive us and then promise never to do it again. Allah is All-Forgiving and All-Kind to the people that ask for His forgiveness and He increases their blessings.

THE KIND KING

Al-Kahf 18:83-98

While there have been many rulers in history who have been wicked and oppressed good people, like the Pharaoh, the Qu'ran also tells us stories of good and wise rulers who can also teach us a lot of lessons by their good deeds. This is the story of one such kind king called Dhul Qarnain.

Once upon a time, there was a good and wise king whose name was Dhul Qarnain. Allah ﷻ had given him a lot of power and a big country to rule. One day he decided to travel to the West of his kingdom, to the land of the setting sun. He kept on travelling until he reached an ocean. He could only see dark water and the sun setting on the other side. There he met some people who were disobeying the commands of Allah ﷻ.

Allah ﷻ said to him, "O Dhul Qarnain! You have full power over these people. You can either punish them or be kind to them."

Dhul Qarnain said, "I will only punish those people who do wrong things. And when they die, Allah ﷻ will punish them more on the Day of Judgement. But I will be kind to those people who believe in Allah ﷻ and do good things. And when they die, Allah ﷻ will give them good reward on the Day of Judgement."

After sorting out these people, Dhul Qarnain set off to the East. He kept on travelling until he reached the land of the rising sun. There he saw some people who had no protection from the sun. They lived a simple life and did not need many things. Dhul Qarnain did not interfere with their way of life and set off on his travels again.

He kept on travelling until he reached an area between two mountains. The people living on one side of the mountain could hardly understand his language, but through interpreters, they said to Dhul Qarnain, "O Dhul Qarnain, the people of Gog and Magog live on the other of the mountains. They are bad people and they are making our lives difficult. If you could build a wall between us then we would be very grateful to you and we will pay you."

Dhul Qarnain said, "Allah ﷻ has given me enough money and power, so I do not need your payment. But if you could help me with the work then I can build a wall for you. You can start by bringing me some blocks of iron."

With these blocks of iron, Dhul Qarnain built a wall between the two mountains. When it had been built, Dhul Qarnain asked the people to heat up the wall and asked them to bring him some molten lead. He used this to fill the gaps in the iron wall. This made the wall very strong and no one could climb up it, destroy it or dig through it.

Once the job was finished, Dhul Qarnain took no credit for his hard work and said, "This is a mercy from Allah ﷻ. But a time will come when this wall will break down. This is the promise of Allah ﷻ. The promise of Allah ﷻ is always true."

LESSONS TO BE LEARNED

- Although Dhul Qarnain was king, he knew that this responsibility was a gift from Allah ﷻ. He was not proud or arrogant about it, but used his money and power wisely. He knew that he would have to answer to Allah ﷻ about how he used his wealth and power. If we are given money or power then we should remember that it is a blessing from Allah ﷻ and that we will have to answer to Allah ﷻ about how we used it.

- Dhul Qarnain was a helpful king. Instead of sitting in a luxurious palace with servants all around him, he travelled throughout his kingdom, to find how he could help people. We should also try to found out how we can help people around us and make them happy.

- Because Dhul Qarnain was a good Muslim king, he only punished those people who did wrong things according to the commands of Allah ﷻ when he visited the land of the setting sun. He did not make up his own laws and rules.

- Dhul Qarnain protected his people from the bad tribes of Gog and Magog by building a wall. Similarly, we should also not encourage bad behaviour. If we see something that goes against the commands of Allah ﷻ, then we should either try to stop it politely or we should protect people from it.

- If we help someone, we should not take credit for it or boast about it to other people or ask for something in return. Helping other people is our duty and Allah ﷻ will reward us for it, insha'Allah.

The Queen of Saba

Al-Naml 27:16-44

Sulayman عليه السلام was another good and wise king as well as being a prophet of Allah ﷻ. He used his position to invite the Queen of another country, Saba, to accept Islam in a very clever way.

Sulayman عليه السلام was a prophet of Allah ﷻ, the son of another great prophet, Dawud عليه السلام. Allah ﷻ had made Sulayman عليه السلام a great ruler and blessed him with much wealth. In Sulayman's عليه السلام army, there were men, Jinns and birds. Allah ﷻ had also given Sulayman عليه السلام the ability to understand the language of the birds so he could talk to them as well as listen to what they were saying.

One day, the army was marching through the land and were nearing a valley of ants. One of the ants said to the other ants, "O ants, let us go underground into our homes quickly before Sulayman and his army crush us underneath their feet without realising it."

Sulayman ﷺ heard what the little ant had said, smiled and prayed, "O Allah! May I always be grateful for Your favours, which You have given me and to my parents. May I always do what pleases You so that You will be pleased with me."

One day, while Sulayman ﷺ was checking his army of birds, he noticed that one of the birds was missing. He said, "How come I do not see the Hud Hud? Why is he absent? If he cannot give me a good explanation, then I will punish him or slaughter him."

As it happened, the Hud Hud was not far away and soon he came and said to Sulayman ﷺ, "I have just returned from a country which you have not seen called Saba. It is ruled by a woman who sits on a magnificent throne and she lives in luxury. But she and her people do not worship Allah ﷻ, they worship the Sun. Shaytan has misguided them so that they cannot see what they are doing wrong by not worshipping Allah ﷻ alone, Who knows what is hidden in the Heavens and the Earth. He knows anything we try to hide or show off. There is no god except Allah ﷻ. His throne is the most magnificent throne."

Having listened to the Hud Hud intently, Sulayman عليه السلام said, "Let me find out if you are telling the truth. Take this letter to the Queen of Saba, and then watch what she does with it."

The Hud Hud took Sulayman's عليه السلام letter and dropped it in front of the Queen. The Queen opened the letter, read it, and then said to her people, "O people! I have here an important letter. It is from Sulayman and it reads as follows:

> '*Bismillahir Rahmanir Raheem*! (In the name of Allah, Most Kind, Most Merciful). I invite you to accept the true religion of Islam and do not be arrogant.'"

After reading the letter, the Queen asked her advisers, "O chiefs! I need your advice. I have never made any decision without your advice."

They said, "We are tough and powerful. Just give us the order and we will fight him."

The Queen thought for a while and then said, "Fighting is not good. When an army invades a country, it destroys cities and makes its people slaves. If Sulayman wanted to conquer us, he could have invaded, but instead he has sent me a letter. Let me send my ambassadors to Sulayman with a present and then see what he does."

The Queen's ambassadors came to Sulayman عليه السلام, offering him gifts from the Queen of Saba. Sulayman عليه السلام looked at these and said to the ambassadors, "You are offering me expensive gifts and money. But Allah ﷻ has given me better than this. You may be happy that you have all this wealth, so you can take it back with you. I will come to your country with my army, which is so big that you will not be able to fight back."

The ambassadors returned to the Queen still carrying the gifts and gave Sulayman's عليه السلام message to her.

Meanwhile, Sulayman ﷺ had an idea. He said to his army, "O chiefs, can you bring me the Queen's throne as quickly as possible?"

Ifrit, a large and powerful Jinn, said, "I can bring it to you before you can get up from your seat. I am very strong and trustworthy."

Then someone who was more knowledgeable about religion said, "I can bring you the throne within the blink of an eye." Indeed, as soon as he had spoken, the throne was right in front of Sulayman's ﷺ eyes.

When Sulayman ﷺ saw the throne in front of him, he said, "This is by the grace of Allah ﷻ. It is a test from Him, to see whether I am thankful to Him or not. If anyone gives thanks to Allah ﷻ, it is only for his own good and if he does not give thanks to Allah ﷻ, then it makes no difference to Allah ﷻ, because Allah ﷻ does not need anyone's thanks."

Sulayman عليه السلام then ordered a Jinn, "Change the Queen's throne so much that she is no longer able to recognise it. If she can recognise her throne even then, then she will have to accept that this is a miracle of Allah ﷻ and then she will accept Islam."

When the Queen arrived, she was asked, "Is this your throne?"

The Queen replied, "It is just like mine."

She was then invited to enter Sulayman's عليه السلام palace. But at the entrance, she thought there was a pool of water and lifted up her skirt to prevent her clothes getting wet.

Sulayman عليه السلام reassured her and said, "This is not a pool of water but a floor made of glass."

The Queen realised that these were miracles of Allah ﷻ and said, humbly, "O Allah! I have been unjust to myself. I submit to You, the Lord of the Universe, in Islam."

Sulayman عليه السلام was thankful to Allah ﷻ that the Queen had the good sense to recognise the miracles of Allah ﷻ and accept Islam.

LESSONS TO BE LEARNED

● Sulayman ﷺ was a great and powerful ruler with a huge army and yet he was careful not to hurt even the tiny ants that were on the ground.

● Sulayman ﷺ was not proud and arrogant because of what Allah ﷻ had blessed him with and he always remembered that this was a grace from Allah ﷻ. He prayed and thanked Allah ﷻ when he heard the little ant and he also prayed and thanked Allah ﷻ when the Queen's throne was brought before him. We should always remember and thank Allah ﷻ as often as possible for all His blessings which are too many to count.

● Everything worships and praises Allah ﷻ – people, Jinns and animals alike. Even the Hud Hud bird knew that people should worship Allah ﷻ alone. Even the bird knew that Shaytan is our greatest enemy and will always try to mislead us. So we should always be careful that we are not doing *shirk*, making other things equal to Allah ﷻ.

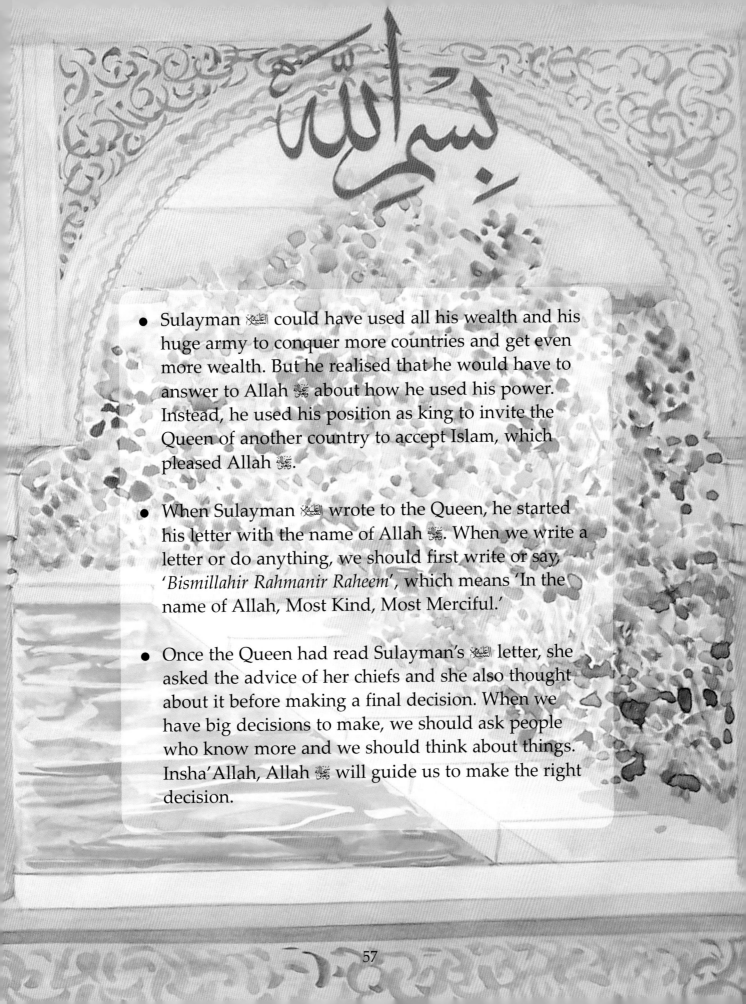

- Sulayman ﷺ could have used all his wealth and his huge army to conquer more countries and get even more wealth. But he realised that he would have to answer to Allah ﷻ about how he used his power. Instead, he used his position as king to invite the Queen of another country to accept Islam, which pleased Allah ﷻ.

- When Sulayman ﷺ wrote to the Queen, he started his letter with the name of Allah ﷻ. When we write a letter or do anything, we should first write or say, *'Bismillahir Rahmanir Raheem'*, which means 'In the name of Allah, Most Kind, Most Merciful.'

- Once the Queen had read Sulayman's ﷺ letter, she asked the advice of her chiefs and she also thought about it before making a final decision. When we have big decisions to make, we should ask people who know more and we should think about things. Insha'Allah, Allah ﷻ will guide us to make the right decision.

- Sulayman عليه السلام refused to accept the expensive gifts from the Queen. Accepting the gifts would have meant that he was interested in money, but it was more important for Sulayman عليه السلام to invite the Queen to Islam. It is much more important to do good deeds and help other people than it is to make money.

- Although Sulayman عليه السلام had a huge army and could fight with the people of Saba, he first decided to invite the Queen to accept Islam by using her intelligence. There are so many wonders and miracles of Allah ﷻ all around us that any intelligent person will accept Islam by thinking about these. The

Queen was an intelligent lady and was able to understand and accept Islam.

- The Queen of Saba was a guest of Sulayman ﷺ and he treated her with respect and kindness, even though she was not a Muslim. We should also be kind and respectful to our guests when they visit us.

- Like us, Jinns are also servants of Allah ﷺ. They are made out of fire, while human beings are made out of clay. They can see us but we cannot see them. There are good Jinns who worship Allah ﷺ and do good deeds and there are also bad Jinns, such as Shaytan, who mislead people. There are lots of things that Jinns can do that we cannot do, like changing shape and travelling faster than we do. This is all by the permission of Allah ﷺ.

ALLAH IS MY LORD

Al-An'am 6:74-82

Another very wise and intelligent person was the Prophet Ibrahim ﷺ. There are many stories about him in the Qur'an as he is a very important prophet. In fact, the Prophet Muhammad ﷺ was descended from the Prophet Ibrahim ﷺ. The following is a story from when Ibrahim ﷺ was a young man.

Ibrahim ﷺ was a very intelligent person. He was born among people who worshipped idols and made them equal to Allah ﷻ. This is called *shirk*, which is the worst sin in Islam. Ibrahim ﷺ, however, realised that he should not worship the idols. After all they were made of stone and could not actually do anything.

So one day, Ibrahim ﷺ said to his father, Azar, "Why do you worship idols? I think that you and your people are making a big mistake."

When Azar did not take much notice of what his son said, Ibrahim ﷺ thought about what he could worship instead of idols.

That night, Ibrahim ﷻ saw a star twinkling in the sky and said, "This is my Lord." But when the star disappeared, he said, "I do not love things that disappear."

When he saw the moon, shining brighter than anything else in the night sky, he said, "This is my Lord." But again when the moon set, he realised that this was not an object of worship and said, "Unless my Lord guides me then I will be a loser."

In the morning, Ibrahim ﷻ saw the sun rising brightly over the horizon. He said, "This is my Lord. This is shining more brightly than anything I have ever seen!" But again that evening the sun set and he realised that none of these things could be worshipped.

In this way, Allah ﷻ had shown Ibrahim ﷻ the objects in the Heavens and Earth and guided him. Now Ibrahim ﷻ understood that none of these objects were gods. His Lord was actually the One Who had made all of these things.

He cried out, "O my people! I have nothing to do with the things you make equal to Allah . From now on I will only worship Allah Who made the Heavens and Earth. I shall never make anything equal to Allah."

His people did not like what he had to say and started arguing with him. They also tried to frighten him by telling him what would happen if he did not follow the way that everybody follows.

Ibrahim ﷵ replied, "Are you arguing with me about Allah ﷻ Who has guided me? I am not afraid of the things you call god, they cannot hurt me. Nothing can happen to me except what Allah ﷻ commands. He is the All-Knowing. Why should I be scared of the things you have made god, when you are not afraid of Allah ﷻ? Do you have any proof of what you believe in? Now tell me something: Who should feel safer? The one who only worships Allah ﷻ or the one who worships idols?"

They had no answer. So Ibrahim ﷵ himself replied, "Of course, the one who worships only Allah ﷻ."

LESSONS TO BE LEARNED

- When Ibrahim ﷿ saw his people worshipping idols, he did not automatically follow them because that is what everyone was doing. First he asked himself, "Does it make sense?" We should always use our intelligence and common sense when we do things. We should ask ourselves, "Is it permitted by Allah ﷻ and the Prophet Muhammad ﷺ?" We should not just copy other people.

- When we use our intelligence and try to do things that please Allah ﷻ, then Allah ﷻ helps us and guides us in the right direction, just as He guided Ibrahim ﷿ to the Right Way.

- Once we understand the reason for doing something and know that it is the right thing to do, then we should do it without being afraid of anyone or anything except Allah ﷻ. Once Ibrahim ﷿ understood why he should only worship Allah ﷻ, he was not afraid to tell his people what he believed in.

- Worshipping and believing in Allah alone makes a person brave. When a person believes in Allah ﷻ, He gives him guidance. This is what happened with Ibrahim ﷺ. He became a brave person when he started believing in Allah ﷻ. He was not afraid to say what was right to his people. He was not afraid to tell them that they were wrong in doing *shirk*.

- When we do something that is different from what other people are doing, then they may make fun of us, argue with us or try to change our mind. If we are following the commands of Allah ﷻ and His Prophet ﷺ then we should carry on what we are doing without worrying about other people. We should only care what Allah ﷻ thinks and about pleasing Allah ﷻ.

THE TOUGHEST TEST

As-Saffat 37:100-111

We saw that Ibrahim ﷺ warned his people that they were not doing the right thing. However, his people did not listen to him and made his life very difficult. Finally, he decided to leave his home and move away for the sake of Allah ﷻ. He went to Syria and Palestine and here we continue, when he is now an old man.

When Ibrahim ﷺ was settled in Syria and Palestine, he was an old man and still did not have any children. So he prayed to Allah ﷻ, "O my Lord! Give me a good and righteous son."

Allah ﷻ accepted his prayer and gave him the good news that he would have a gentle and patient son. His name was Isma'il.

Many years passed and Isma'il ﷺ was now a young man. One day, Ibrahim ﷺ said to him, "O my son! I saw in my dream that I must sacrifice you. What do you think?"

Isma'il ﷺ replied, "O my father! You must do as Allah ﷻ orders you. Insha'Allah, you will find out that I have lot of patience."

They both decided to do what Allah ﷻ wanted them to do. Ibrahim ﷺ laid Isma'il ﷺ on the ground in the *sajdah* position and got ready to sacrifice his son.

When Ibrahim ﷺ was about to sacrifice Isma'il ﷺ, Allah ﷻ called out to him and said, "O Ibrahim! You made your dream come true. This was only a test for you. This was only to increase the reward of those who do the right thing."

Allah ﷻ placed a sheep where Isma'il ﷺ was lying and Ibrahim ﷺ sacrificed the sheep instead.

Allah ﷻ left a good name for Ibrahim ﷺ among future generations: Peace be upon Ibrahim ﷺ.

LESSONS TO BE LEARNED

- Ibrahim ﷺ prayed to Allah ﷻ to grant him a good Muslim son, even though he was an old man. We should not give up hope and always keep praying to Allah ﷻ, no matter how unlikely it seems that our prayers can be granted. Remember that Allah ﷻ can do anything.

- Ibrahim ﷺ was a good and righteous man who prayed for a good thing so Allah ﷻ answered his prayer. We should also try our best to please Allah ﷻ in our lives so Allah ﷻ will answer our prayers and we should always pray for good things.

- Ibrahim ﷺ was ready to follow the commands of Allah ﷻ even if it meant sacrificing his son, whom he loved very much. We should also be ready to give up those things that we love and really want, to please Allah ﷻ. Maybe our parents have given us some money so that we can buy something that we really want. But it would please Allah ﷻ if we gave some of that money to poor people and not buy the thing we really want.

- Ibrahim ﷺ was given a big test from Allah ﷻ and he passed that test. In the same way, we are given tests by Allah ﷻ to see if we will pass. If we do pass, then Allah ﷻ will give us more good things in this life and insha'Allah a place in Paradise. For example, imagine it is time for Maghrib Prayer and at the same time there is a good programme on TV. Allah is testing us: do we pray or keep on watching the programme? If we turn the TV off and pray, we have passed this test. If someone is rude to us, this is a test from Allah ﷻ. Are we rude back to that person or do we behave nicely and politely because we are good Muslims? If we behave politely then we have passed the test.

- When Ibrahim ﷺ asked his son if he would be sacrificed for the sake of Allah ﷻ, Isma'il ﷺ happily agreed. When our parents ask us to do something which is not against Islam, we should happily do it.

- When we face a hard time, we should be patient. It could be a test from Allah ﷻ. If we show patience, Allah ﷻ will reward us more. Allah ﷻ rewarded Ibrahim ﷺ by telling his good actions to us and keeping his act of sacrifice alive. Every year at Eid-ul-Adha, we also sacrifice an animal and eat and distribute the meat in order to remember the sacrifice of Ibrahim ﷺ.

WORDS OF WISDOM

Luqman 31:12-19

A long time ago, there was a very wise man called Luqman. The thirty-first Surah of the Qur'an is named after him. He was not a Prophet but Allah ﷻ granted him with intelligence and understanding. He left his son his some of words of wisdom and we will end the stories with these very important lessons.

- We should be grateful to Allah ﷻ. Whoever is grateful to Allah ﷻ, it is for his own good. Allah ﷻ does not need anyone to be grateful to Him. If we are not grateful to Allah ﷻ then we only harm ourselves.

- We should not worship anything else apart from Allah ﷻ. This is the biggest sin and is called *shirk*. We must have full trust in Allah ﷻ and not on any other person or object.

- Allah ﷻ asks people to be good and kind to their parents. He reminds us that our mothers have sacrificed so much to bring us into this world and to feed us, so we should be grateful, firstly to Allah ﷻ and then to our parents. The only time we can disobey our parents is when they ask us to do something against Allah ﷻ and Islam.

- Allah ﷻ knows about everything in the entire universe even if it is as small as a seed hidden in a rock anywhere in the heavens or on earth. We cannot hide our bad deeds from Allah ﷻ. But on the other hand whatever good we do, Allah ﷻ knows about it and He will make sure that we are rewarded.

- It is important to pray regularly five times a day. We should always speak the truth and speak out against what is wrong. We should be patient whatever happens. All these things are signs of good faith and will please Allah ﷻ.

- Allah ﷻ does not like people who are proud or arrogant. We must never think that we are better than other people.

- Everything we do should be moderate. That means that we should not be silent and we should not talk too much. We should not be too proud and we should not be too shy. We should not shout or raise our voice to anyone because that is a sound that Allah ﷻ does not like.

بِسْمِ اللهِ الرَّحْمٰنِ الرَّحِيمِ

اللّٰهُمَّ اٰنِسْ وَحْشَتِى فِى قَبْرِى اللّٰهُمَّ ارْحَمْنِى
بِالْقُرْاٰنِ الْعَظِيمِ وَاجْعَلْهُ لِى اِمَامًا وَّنُوْرًا وَّ
هُدًى وَّرَحْمَةً اللّٰهُمَّ ذَكِّرْنِى مِنْهُ مَا
نَسِيْتُ وَعَلِّمْنِى مِنْهُ مَاجَهِلْتُ وَارْزُقْنِى
تِلَاوَتَهُ اٰنَاءَ الَّيْلِ وَ اٰنَاءَ النَّهَارِ وَاجْعَلْهُ
لِى حُجَّةً يَارَبَّ الْعٰلَمِيْنَ (اٰمِين)

In the name of Allah, the Most Kind, the Most Merciful.
O Allah, change my fear in my grave to love. O Allah, have mercy on
me in the name of the Great Qur'an and make it for me a guide and
light and guidance and mercy. O Allah, make me remember what of it I
have forgotten, make me know of it that which I have become ignorant
of and make me recite it in the hours of the night and day and make it
an argument for me, O Lord of all the worlds. Ameen.